Invasive Exotic Plant Monitoring at Big Spring Pines Natural Area, Chubb Hollow, Long Bay Field and Long Bay at Ozark National Scenic Riverways

Year 1 (2009)

Natural Resource Technical Report NPS/HTLN/NRTR—2010/290

Mary F. Short, Craig C. Young, Chad S. Gross, and Jennifer L. Haack
National Park Service
Heartland I&M Network
Wilson's Creek National Battlefield
6424 West Farm Road 182, Republic, MO 65738

Heartland Network

Natural Resource Monitoring

February 2010

U.S. Department of the Interior
National Park Service
Natural Resource Program Center
Fort Collins, Colorado

The National Park Service, Natural Resource Program Center publishes a range of reports that address natural resource topics of interest and applicability to a broad audience in the National Park Service and others in natural resource management, including scientists, conservation and environmental constituencies, and the public.

The Natural Resource Technical Report Series is used to disseminate results of scientific studies in the physical, biological, and social sciences for both the advancement of science and the achievement of the National Park Service mission. The series provides contributors with a forum for displaying comprehensive data that are often deleted from journals because of page limitations.

All manuscripts in the series receive the appropriate level of peer review to ensure that the information is scientifically credible, technically accurate, appropriately written for the intended audience, and designed and published in a professional manner. Data in this report were collected and analyzed using methods based on established, peer-reviewed protocols and were analyzed and interpreted within the guidelines of the protocols.

Views, statements, findings, conclusions, recommendations, and data in this report are those of the author(s) and do not necessarily reflect views and policies of the National Park Service, U.S. Department of the Interior. Mention of trade names or commercial products does not constitute endorsement or recommendation for use by the National Park Service.

This report is available from the Heartland I&M Network website (http://www.nature.nps.gov/im/units/HTLN) and the Natural Resource Publications Management website (http://www.nature.nps.gov/publications/NRPM).

Please cite this publication as:

Short, M. F., C. C. Young, C. S. Gross, and J. L. Haack. 2010. Invasive exotic plant monitoring at Big Spring Pines Natural Area, Chubb Hollow, Long Bay Field and Long Bay at Ozark National Scenic Riverways: Year 1 (2010). Natural Resource Technical Report NPS/HTLN/NRTR—2010/290. National Park Service, Fort Collins, Colorado.

NPS 614/101124, February 2010

Contents

Figures

Tables

Abstract

During surveys in 2009, we documented seven invasive exotic plant taxa in the Big Spring Pines Natural Area, Chubb Hollow, Long Bay Field and Long Bay at Ozark National Scenic Riverways. All species were known to occur on the park. The most widespread and abundant of the exotic plant species observed included Johnsongrass, ground ivy and Nepalase browntop. Each of these species covered seven or more acres in the park. In general, several invasive exotic plants are a major problem in the study area at Ozark National Scenic Riverways, but successful control is possible for a large group of species. The acreage estimates presented in the report may be used to plan management activities leading to control of exotic plants and the accomplishment of GPRA goal IA1b.

Introduction

Author's note. In this report, we use the term invasive exotic plant to refer to plants that are not native to the park and that are presumed to pose environmental harm to native plant populations and/or communities based on a review of numerous state and regional invasive exotic plant lists. The great majority of the introductory text was taken from Welch and Geissler (2007) with slight modification.

Scope of invasive exotic plant problem for National Parks

Globalization of commerce, transportation, human migration, and recreation in recent history has introduced invasive exotic species to new areas at an unprecedented rate. Biogeographical barriers that once restricted the location and expansion of species have been circumvented, culminating in the homogenization of the Earth's biota. Although only 10% of introduced species become established and only 1% become problematic (Williamson 1993, Williamson and Fitter 1996) or invasive, nonnative species have profound impacts worldwide on the environment, economies, and human health. Invasive species have been directly linked to the replacement of dominant native species (Tilman 1999), the loss of rare species (King 1985), changes in ecosystem structure, alteration of nutrient cycles and soil chemistry (Ehrenfeld 2003), shifts in community productivity (Vitousek 1990), reduced agricultural productivity, and changes in water availability (D'Antonio and Mahall 1991). Often the damage caused by these species to natural resources is irreparable and our understanding of the consequences incomplete. Invasive species are second only to habitat destruction as a threat to wildland biodiversity (Wilcove et al. 1998). Consequently, the dynamic relationships among plants, animals, soil, and water established over many thousands of years are at risk of being destroyed in a relatively brief period.

For the National Park Service (NPS), the consequences of these invasions present a significant challenge to manage the agency's natural resources "unimpaired for the enjoyment of future generations." National Parks, like other land management organizations, are deluged by new exotic species arriving through predictable (e.g., road, trail, and riparian corridors), sudden (e.g., long-distance dispersal through cargo containers and air freight), and unexpected anthropogenic pathways (e.g., weed seeds in restoration planting mixes). Nonnative plants claim an estimated 4,600 acres of public lands each year in the United States (Asher and Harmon 1995), significantly altering local flora. For example, exotic plants comprise an estimated 43% and 36% of the flora of the states of Hawaii and New York, respectively (Rejmanek and Randall 1994). Invasive plants infest an estimated 2.6 million acres of the 83 million acres managed by the NPS.

More NPS lands are infested daily despite diligent efforts to curtail the problem. Impacts from invasive species have been realized in most parks, resulting in an expressed need to control existing infestations and restore affected ecosystems. Additionally, there is a growing urgency to be proactive—to protect resources not yet impacted by current and future invasive species (Marler 1998). Invasive exotic species most certainly will continue to be a management priority for the National Parks well into the 21st Century. Invasive exotic plants have been consistently ranked as a top vital sign for long term monitoring as part of the NPS Inventory & Monitoring (I&M) Program. During the vital signs selection process in 2003, Heartland Network parks recognized the need for exotic plant monitoring (DeBacker et al. 2004). Nine parks (CUVA, EFMO, GWCA, HEHO, HOCU, HOME, LIBO, OZAR, PERI) identified invasive exotic plants as their most important management issue, two parks (TAPR, WICR) identified invasive exotic plants as their second most important management issue, and PIPE identified invasive exotic plants as its third most important management issue. During this process, invasive exotic plant monitoring was recognized across all network parks as the most important shared monitoring need.

Prevention and early detection as keys to invasive exotic plant management

Prevention and early detection are the principal strategies for successful invasive exotic plant management. While there is a need for long-term suppression programs to address very high-impact species, eradication efforts are most successful for infestations less than one hectare in size (Rejmanek and Pitcairn 2002). Eradication of infestations larger than 100 hectares is largely unsuccessful, costly, and unsustainable (Rejmanek and Pitcairn 2002). Costs, or impacts, to ecosystem components and processes resulting from invasion also increase dramatically over time, making ecosystem restoration improbable in the later stages of invasion. Further, in their detailed review of the nonnative species problem in the United States, the US Congress, Office of Technology Assessment (1993) stated that the environmental and economic benefits of supporting prevention and early detection initiatives significantly outweigh any incurred costs, with the median benefit-to-cost ratio being 17:1 in favor of being proactive.

Although preventing the introduction of invasive exotic plants is the most successful and preferred strategy for resource managers, the realities of globalization, tight fiscal constraints, and limited staff time guarantee that invaders will get through park borders. Fortunately, invasive exotic plants quite often undergo a lag period between introduction and subsequent colonization of new areas. Managers, then, can take advantage of early detection monitoring to make certain invasive exotic species are found and successfully eradicated before populations become well established.

This strategy requires resource managers to: (1) detect invasive exotic species early (i.e., find a new species or an incipient population of an existing species while the infestation is small (less than 1 hectare), and (2) respond rapidly (i.e., implement appropriate management techniques to eliminate the invasive plant and all of its associated regenerative material).

Invasive exotic plant management at Big Spring Pines Natural Area, Chubb Hollow, Long Bay Field and Long Bay at Ozark National Scenic Riverways

While a complete history of park invasive exotic plant management issues is beyond the scope of this report, a few important highlights are given:

1. Invasive exotic plants, such as Johnsongrass (*Sorghum halepense*), have invaded open agricultural fields in the study area at Ozark National Scenic Riverways.

2. Nepalese browntop (*Microstegium vimineum*) has invaded roadsides and mesic forests in some portions of the study area at Ozark National Scenic Riverways.

3. Disturbed areas within the study area at Ozark National Scenic Riverways, including trails and roadways, support a few invasive exotic plant species of moderate concern (Stroh and Struckhoff 2009). We have observed few invasive plant species, however, within interior forests.

Methods

Watch list
We searched for invasive exotic plants known to occur within the study area at Ozark National Scenic Riverways. We developed our list based on NPSpecies, Stroh and Struckhoff (2009), and contact with Kim Houf, terrestrial ecologist at the park. This approach focused on existing invasions rather potential invasions in order to simplify the survey.

Field methods
Invasive exotic plant species on a designated watch list (Table 1) were sought at Big Spring Natural Area, Chubb Hollow, Long Bay Field and Long Bay at Ozark National Scenic Riverways (Figure 1). Following plant identification training provided by Craig Young, Chad Gross and Mary Short conducted monitoring during August 26-28 and September 1-2, 2009. Assisted by a GPS unit, network staff navigated along contiguous 200 m line transects, identified invasive exotic plants in a 3 m- to 12 m-belt, and attributed a coarse cover value to each species (0=0, 1=0.1-0.9 m^2, 2=1-9.9 m^2, 3=10-49.9 m^2, 4= 50-99.9 m^2, 5=100-499.9 m^2, 6= 499.9-999.9 m^2, and 7 ≥ 1,000 m^2). The widest belt possible given site conditions was used. A total of 89 transects were surveyed; transects 90 - 93 were excluded due to inaccessibility of terrain caused by the presence of a large impassable stream in the Long Bay portion of the study area (Figure 1).

Analytical methods
Data analysis involved simple displays, as well as calculation of plant cover and frequency. The invasive exotic plants encountered within the study area at Ozark National Scenic Riverways were attributed to line transects in a GIS (Figures 2 – 8). Note that entire search units were not fully searched. A park-wide cover range was estimated for each invasive exotic plant encountered.

We calculated the observed reference frame fraction by multiplying transect length, the number of transects, and the belt width. The belt width was either 3 m (the minimum possible width) or 12 m (the maximum possible width). The product was then divided by the reference frame area (Eq. 1). We calculated transect lengths using the mean sample unit size and assuming square search units.

Eq. 1. Fraction of area searched = $\dfrac{transect\ length * number\ of\ transects * belt\ width}{reference\ frame\ area}$

The minimum fraction of area searched (belt width = 3 m) was 0.015, and the maximum fraction of area searched (belt width = 12 m) was 0.06.

To calculate the minimum end of the estimated cover range for each species, we summed the lower endpoints associated with the assigned cover class values for that species and then divided by the reference frame fraction observed assuming the widest possible survey belt (i.e., maximum fraction observed) (12 m) (Eq. 2).

Eq. 2. Minimum cover estimate = $\dfrac{\Sigma\ low\ end\ of\ cover\ value\ range\ for\ species}{fraction\ of\ area\ searched\ assuming\ 12\text{-}m\ belt\ width}$

Maximum cover for each species was calculated similarly, using the upper endpoints of the cover values in each occupied search unit and assuming that a 3 m belt was surveyed (i.e., minimum fraction of area observed) (Eq. 3).

$$\text{Eq. 3. Maximum cover estimate} = \frac{\Sigma \text{ high end of cover value range for species}}{\text{fraction of area searched assuming 3-m belt width}}$$

Taken together, the minimum and maximum cover estimates provide an estimated range of cover that accounts for the uncertainty arising from the sampling method. Non-overlapping ranges represent the strongest evidence for differences in abundance.

The park-wide frequency of invasive exotic plants was calculated as the percentage of occupied search units (Eq. 4).

$$\text{Eq. 4. Frequency of an IEP species} = \frac{\Sigma \text{ units occupied by species}}{\Sigma \text{ units sampled}} \text{ X100}$$

Invasiveness ranks.

To provide additional information on the ecological impact and feasibility of control, the ecological impact and general management difficulty sub-ranks that constitute the invasiveness rank (I-rank), as determined by NatureServe (Morse et al. 2004), were listed when available. The ecological impact characterizes the effect of the plant on ecosystem processes, community composition and structure, native plant and animal populations, and the conservation significance of threatened biodiversity. General management difficulty ranks are assigned based on the resources and time generally required to control a plant, the non-target effects of control on native populations, and the accessibility of invaded sites. Sub-ranks are given as high (H), medium (M), low (L), insignificant (I), unknown (U), or a combination of ranks.

Results and Discussion

In 2009, a total of 7 invasive exotic plant species were found during the survey at Big Spring Pines Natural Area, Chubb Hollow, Long Bay Field, and Long Bay at Ozark National Scenic Riverways (Table 2). The distribution and abundance of invasive exotic plant species within the study area varied widely. Johnsongrass (*Sorghum halepense*) was the most abundant species observed, occurring on more than 13 acres. Found only along transects intersecting a park road and in the Long Bay field, Johnsongrass occupied 12.4% of the inventory transects. Ground ivy (*Glechoma hederacea*) appeared on a minimum of 9.7 acres with a frequency of 10.1%, and occurred in transects adjacent to the Current River in Long Bay. The third most abundant species, Nepalese browntop (*Microstegium vimineum*), covered over 7 acres and occurred at a frequency of 15.7%. Nepalese browntop was observed in transects along the Current River and transects intersecting a park road. Although only the fourth most abundant species observed, sericea lespedeza (*Lespedeza cuneata*) had the highest frequency: 24.7%. Sericea lespedeza's preference for disturbed habitats likely accounts for the widespread distribution, as well as the occurrence of this species along roadsides and trails in the park. Kentucky bluegrass (*Poa pratensis*) was the only other species with a cover potentially greater than 1 acre. Kentucky bluegrass occurred exclusively in the transects traversing Long Bay Field and had a frequency of 6.7% across the study area. Sweetclover (*Melilotus officinalis*) and multiflora rose (*Rosa*

4

multiflora) were each observed on less than one acre, and both had relatively low frequencies (3.4% and 4.5%, respectively).

The ecological impact of the seven invasive exotic plants observed in 2009 ranged from medium to low/insignificant with most species having a medium ecological impact. Johnsongrass and Nepalese browntop were ranked as species generating high/medium management difficulty; however, the majority of the species are of little management concern with ratings of only medium to low management difficulty. Controlling as many species as possible now should provide a relatively low cost for a high benefit. On the other hand, control of Johnsongrass and Nepalese browntop may prove to be difficult as both grasses are abundant in the park and are difficult to manage.

In summary, this report provides information on invasive, exotic plant abundance and distribution as well as the ecological impacts and management difficulty associated with these species. The information is designed to assist natural resource managers in planning invasive exotic plant management on national parks.

Literature Cited

Asher, J. A., and D. W. Harmon. 1995. Invasive exotic plants are destroying the naturalness of U.S. Wilderness areas. International Journal of Wilderness 1:35-37.

D'Antonio, C. M., and B. E. Mahall. 1991. Root profiles and competition between the invasive, exotic perennial, *Carpobrotus edulis,* and two native shrub species in California coastal scrub. American Journal of Botany 78:885-894.

DeBacker, M. D., C. C. Young (editor), P. Adams, L. Morrison, D. Peitz, G. A. Rowell, M. Williams, and D. Bowles. 2005. Heartland Inventory and Monitoring Network and Prairie Cluster Prototype Monitoring Program Vital Signs Monitoring Plan. National Park Service, Heartland Inventory and Monitoring Network and Prairie Cluster Prototype Monitoring Program, Wilson's Creek National Battlefield, Republic, Missouri, 104 pp. plus appendices.

Ehrenfeld, J. G. 2003. The effects of exotic plant invasions on soil nutrient cycling processes. Ecosystems 6:503-523.

King, W. B. 1985. Island birds: will the future repeat the past? Pages 3-15 *in* P. J. Moors, editor. Conservation of Island Birds. International Council for Bird Preservation. Cambridge University Press, Cambridge, UK.

Marler, M. 1998. Exotic plant invasions of federal Wilderness areas: current status and future directions. The Aldo Leopold Wilderness Research Institute. Rocky Mountain Research Station, Missoula, Montana.

Office of Technology Assessment. 1993. Harmful non-indigenous species in the United States. OTA-F-565. U.S. Congress, Government Printing Office, Washington, D.C.

Rejmanek, M., and M. J. Pitcairn. 2002. When is eradication of exotic pest plants a realistic goal? Pages 249-253 in C. R. Veitch and M. N. Clout, editors. Turning the Tide: the Eradication of Invasive Species. IUCN SSC Invasive Species Specialist Group. IUCN, Gland, Switzerland and Cambridge, UK.

Rejmanek, M., and J. M. Randall. 1994. Invasive alien plants in California: 1993 summary and comparison with other areas in North America. Madrono 41:161–177.

Stroh, E. D., and M. S. Struckhoff. 2009. Exotic plant species associations with horse trails, old roads, and intact native communities in the Missouri Ozarks. Natural Areas Journal 29(1): 50-56.

Tilman, D. 1999. The ecological consequences of changes in biodiversity: a search for general principles. Ecology 80:1455-1474.

Vitousek, P. M. 1990. Biological invasions and ecosystem processes: towards an integration of population biology and ecosystem studies. Oikos 57:7-13.

Welch, B. A. and P. H. Geissler. 2007. Early detection of invasive plants: a handbook. United States Geological Survey draft. Online. (http://www.pwrc.usgs.gov/brd/invasiveHandbook.cfm). Accessed 19 February 2010.

Wilcove, D. S., D. Rothstein, J. Dubow, A. Phillips, and E. Losos. 1998. Quantifying threats to imperiled species in the United States. Bioscience 48:607–615.

Williamson, M. 1993. Invaders, weeds and risk from genetically modified organisms. Experientia 49:219–224.

Williamson, M. and A. Fitter. 1996. The varying success of invaders. Ecology 77:1661–1666.

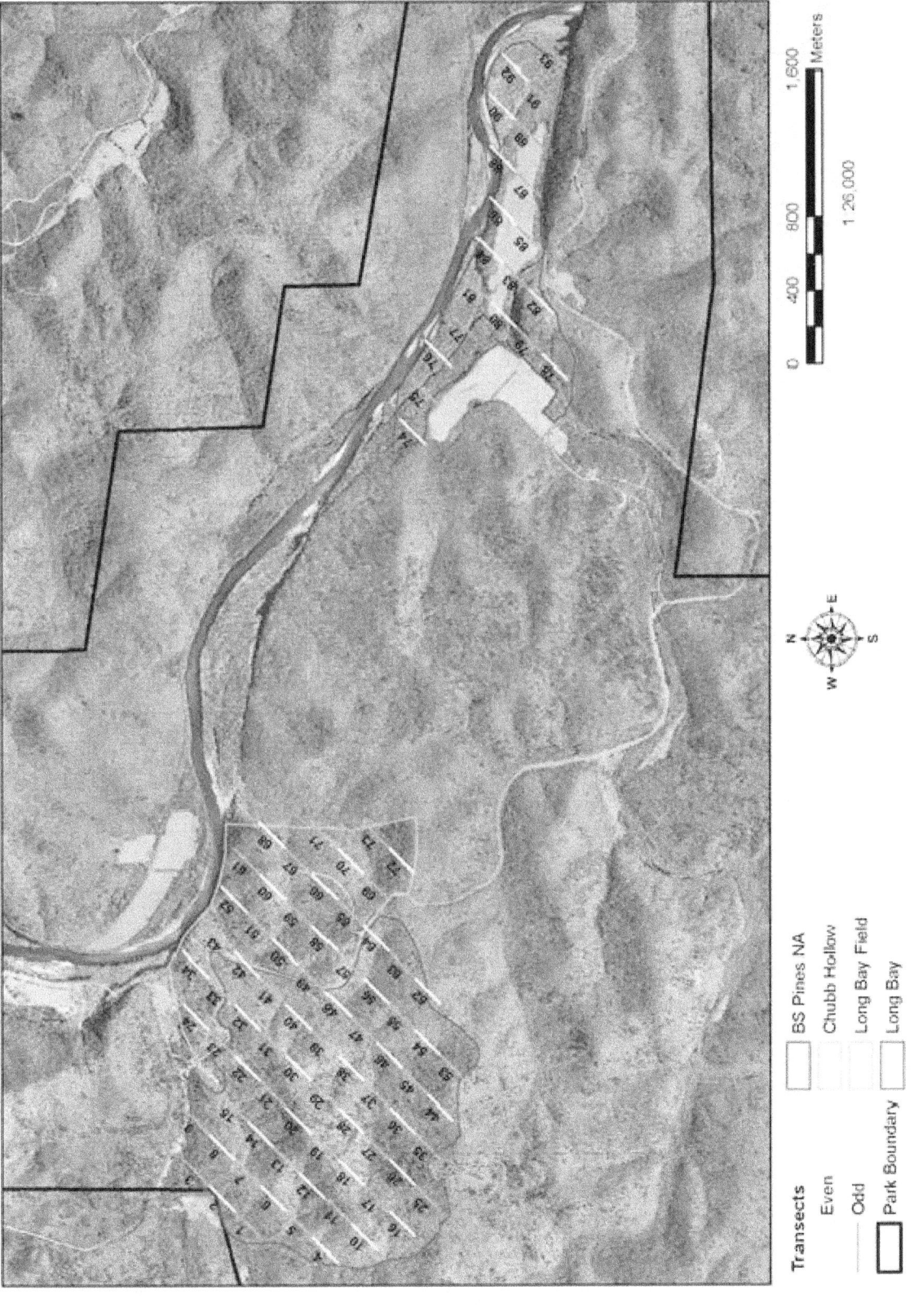

Figure 1. Invasive exotic plant line transects (blue and yellow) at Big Spring Pines Natural Area (BS Pines NA), Chubb Hollow, Long Bay Field, and Long Bay at Ozark National Scenic Riverways. The blue and yellow transects indicate the search locations for invasive exotic plants in 2009.

9

Table 1. Invasive Plant Watch List for Big Spring Pines Natural Area, Chubb Hollow, Long Bay Field, and Long Bay at Ozark National Scenic Riverways.

Scientific Name	Common Name
Albizia julibrissin	Silktree; mimosa
Alliaria petiolata	Garlic mustard
Arctium minus	Lesser burdock
Bromus tectorum	Cheatgrass
Centaurea stoebe ssp. Micranthos	Spotted knapweed
Cirsium vulgare	Bull thistle
Daucus carota	Quenn Ann's lace
Elaeagnus umbellata	Autumn olive
Glechoma hederacea	Ground ivy
Hypericum perforatum	Common St. Johnswort
Leonurus cardiaca	Common motherwort
Lespedeza cuneata	Sericea lespedeza
Lonicera japonica	Japanese honeysuckle
Lysimachia nummularia	Creeping jenny
Maclura pomifera	Osage orange
Melilotus officinalis	Sweetclover
Microstegium vimineum	Nepalese browntop
Morus alba	White mulberry
Poa pratensis	Kentucky bluegrass
Populus alba	White poplar
Potentilla recta	Sulphur cinquefoil
Rhus glabra	Smooth sumac
Robinia pseudoacacia	Black locust
Rosa multiflora	Multiflora rose
Rumex acetosella	Red sorrel; field sorrel
Rumex crispus	Sour dock; curly dock
Saponaria officinalis	Bouncing bet
Securigera varia	Crownvetch
Sorghum halepense	Johnsongrass
Torilis arvensis	Spreading hedgeparsley
Torilis japonica	Erect hedgeparsley
Verbascum thapsus	Common mullein

Table 2. Overview of invasive exotic plants found at Big Spring Pines Natural Area, Chubb Hollow, Long Bay Field, and Long Bay at Ozark National Scenic Riverways in 2009. Ecological impact and general management difficulty based on NatureServe I-Rank subranks, Morse et al. 2004. Subranks are given as high (H), medium (M), low (L), insignificant (I), unknown (U), a range of ranks (indicated by /), or not available.

Scientific Name	Common Name	Watch list	Study Area-wide Cover (acres)	Frequency (Percent)	Ecological impact	Management difficulty
Sorghum halepense	Johnsongrass	Park-established	13.6 - 174.1	12.4	ML	HM
Glechoma hederacea	Ground ivy	Park-established	9.7 - 93.1	10.1	LI	ML
Microstegium vimineum	Nepalese browntop	Park-established	7.1 - 65.4	15.7	M	HM
Lespedeza cuneata	Sericea lespedeza	Park-established	1.4 - 23.3	24.7	M	M
Poa pratensis	Kentucky bluegrass	Park-established	0.4 - 5.8	6.7	M	ML
Melilotus officinalis	Yellow sweetclover	Park-established	< 1.0	3.4	M	M
Rosa multiflora	Multiflora rose	Park-established	< 0.25	4.5	L	L

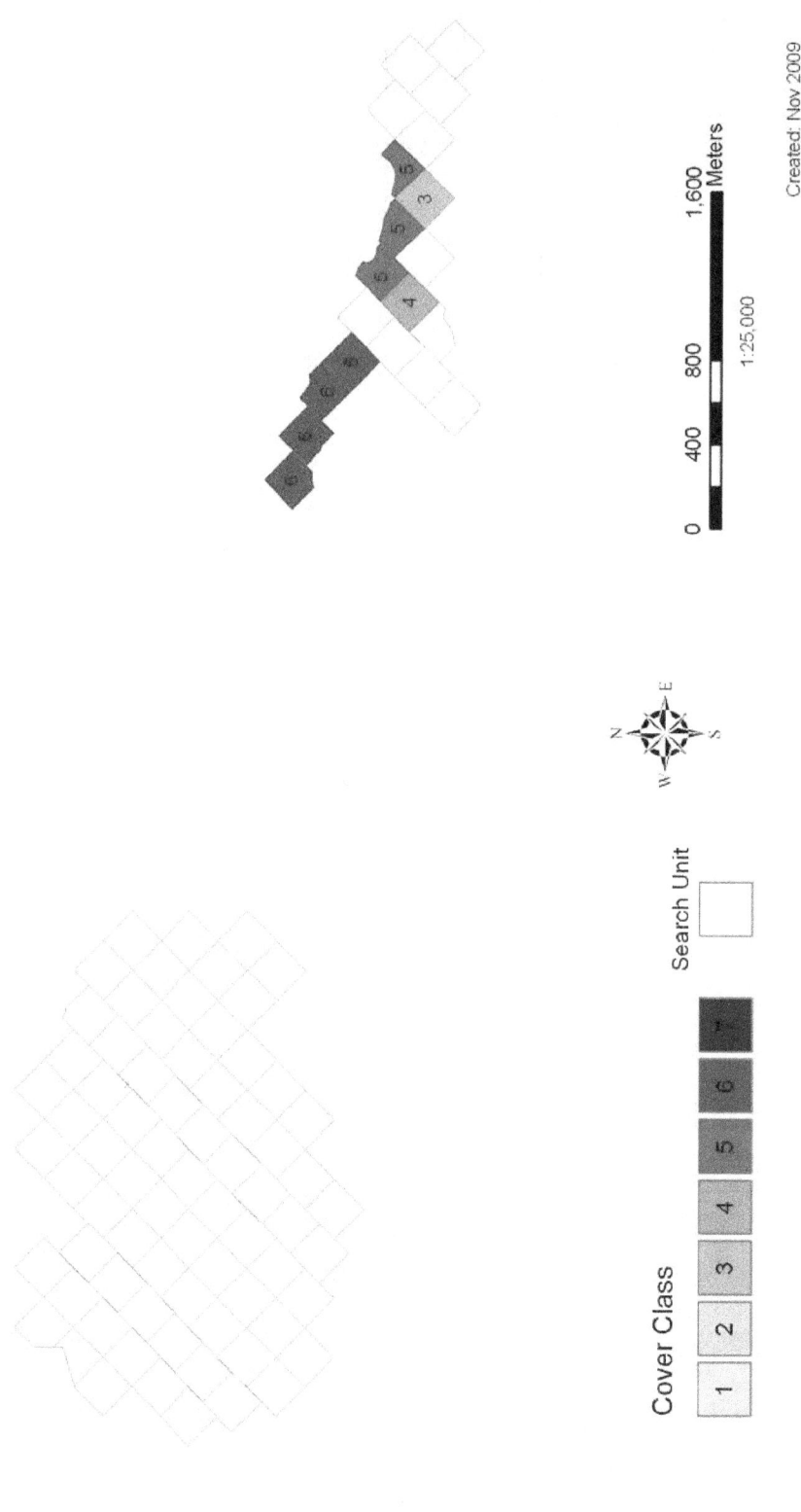

Glechoma hederacea

2009

Cover Class

| 1 | 2 | 3 | 4 | 5 | 6 | 7 |

Search Unit

Created: Nov 2009

0   400   800   1,600
Meters

1:25,000

Figure 2. Abundance and distribution of *Glechoma hederacea* (ground ivy) at Big Spring Pines Natural Area, Chubb Hollow, Long Bay Field, and Long Bay at Ozark National Scenic Riverways, 2009. Cover classes are as follows: 1=0.1-0.9 m², 2=1-9.9 m², 3=10-49.9 m², 4= 50-99.9 m², 5=100-499.9 m², 6= 499.9-999.9 m², and 7 ≥ 1,000 m².

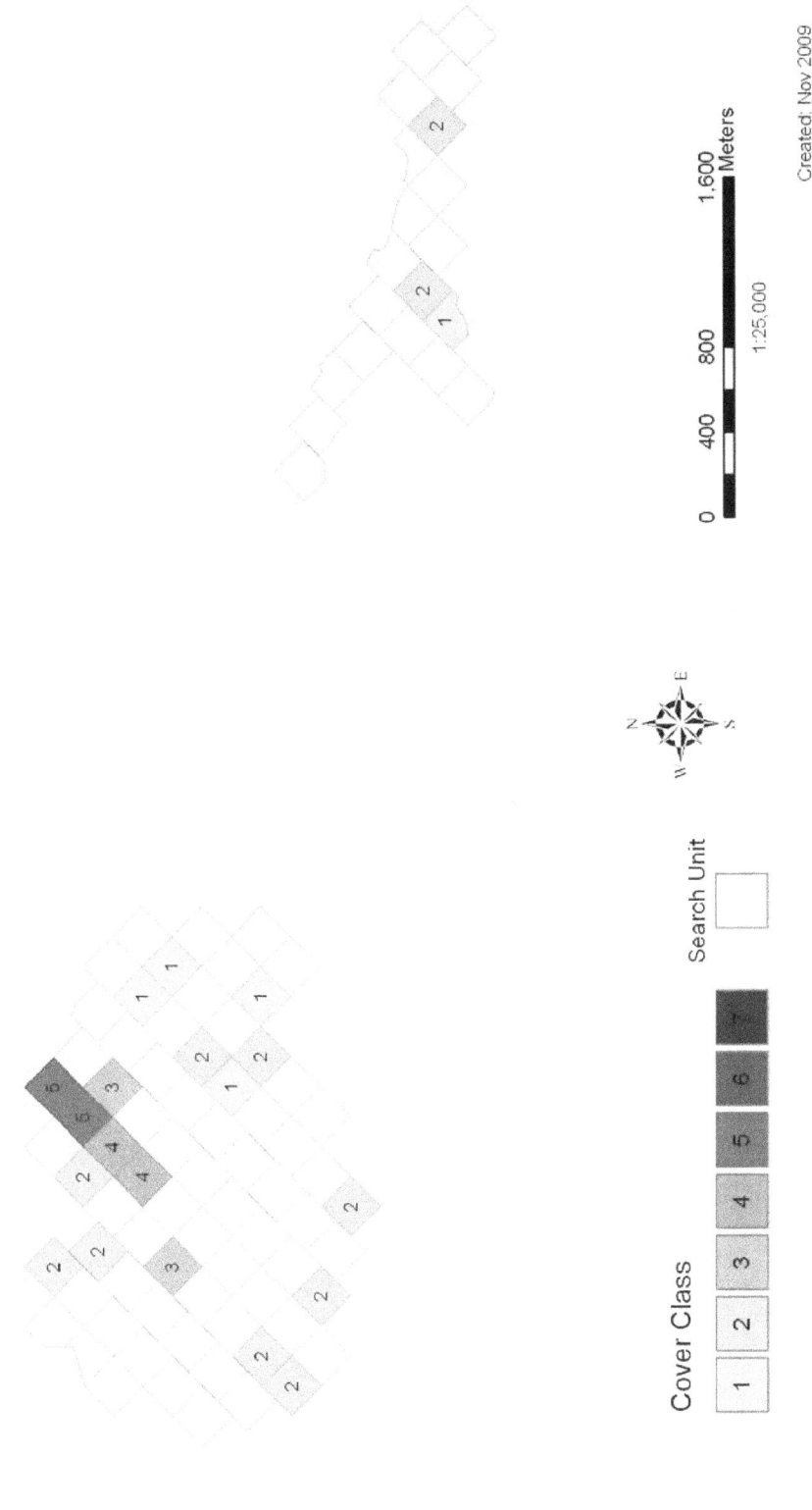

Lespedeza cuneata

2009

Cover Class

Search Unit

Figure 3. Abundance and distribution of *Lespedeza cuneata* (sericea lespedeza) at Big Spring Pines Natural Area, Chubb Hollow, Long Bay Field, and Long Bay at Ozark National Scenic Riverways, 2009. Cover classes are as follows: 1=0.1-0.9 m^2, 2=1-9.9 m^2, 3=10-49.9 m^2, 4= 50-99.9 m^2, 5=100-499.9 m^2, 6= 499.9-999.9 m^2, and 7 ≥ 1,000 m^2.

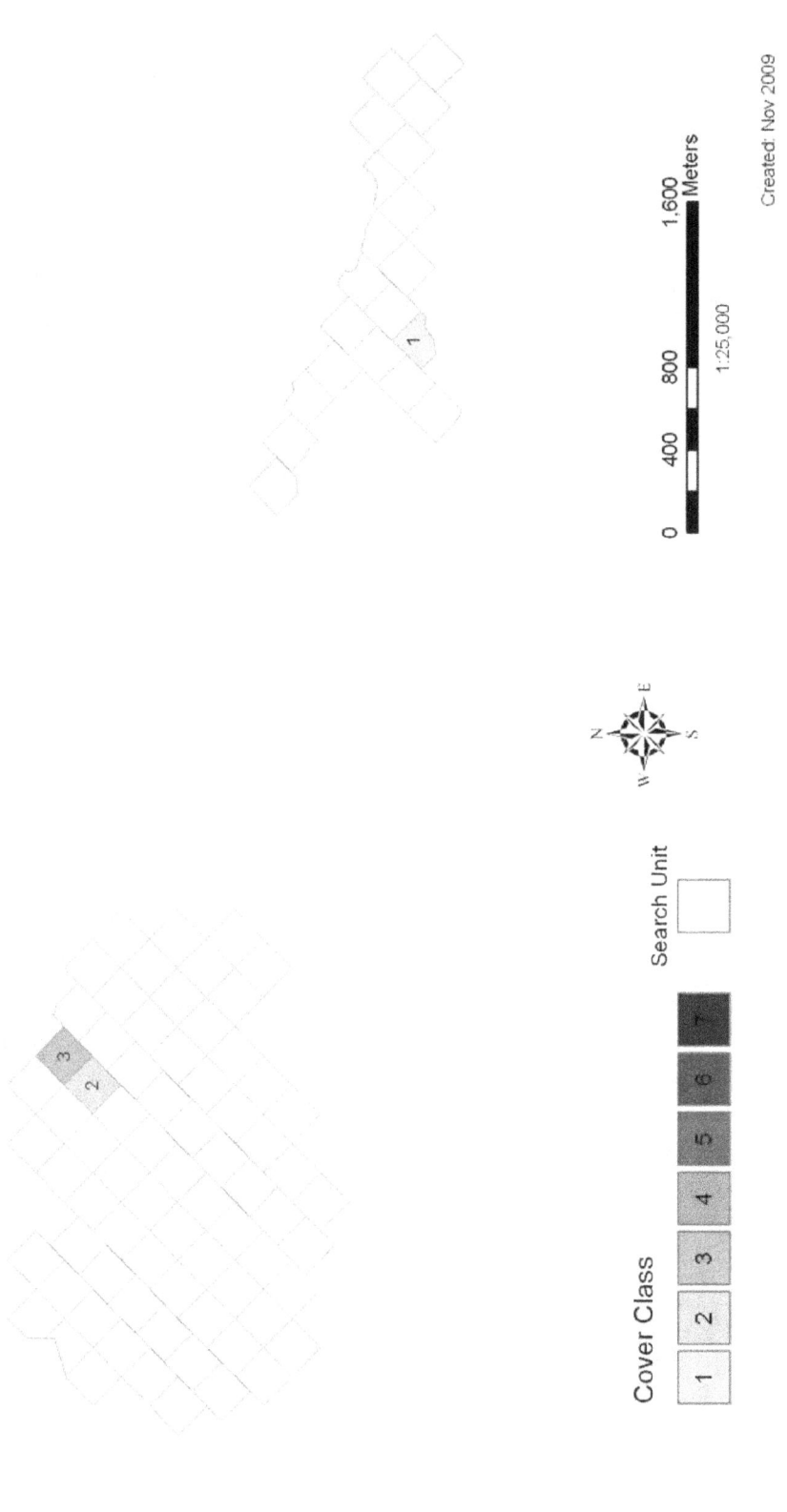

Figure 4. Abundance and distribution of *Melilotus officinalis* (yellow sweetclover) at Big Spring Pines Natural Area, Chubb Hollow, Long Bay Field, and Long Bay at Ozark National Scenic Riverways, 2009. Cover classes are as follows: 1=0.1-0.9 m^2, 2=1-9.9 m^2, 3=10-49.9 m^2, 4= 50-99.9 m^2, 5=100-499.9 m^2, 6= 499.9-999.9 m^2, and 7 ≥ 1,000 m^2.

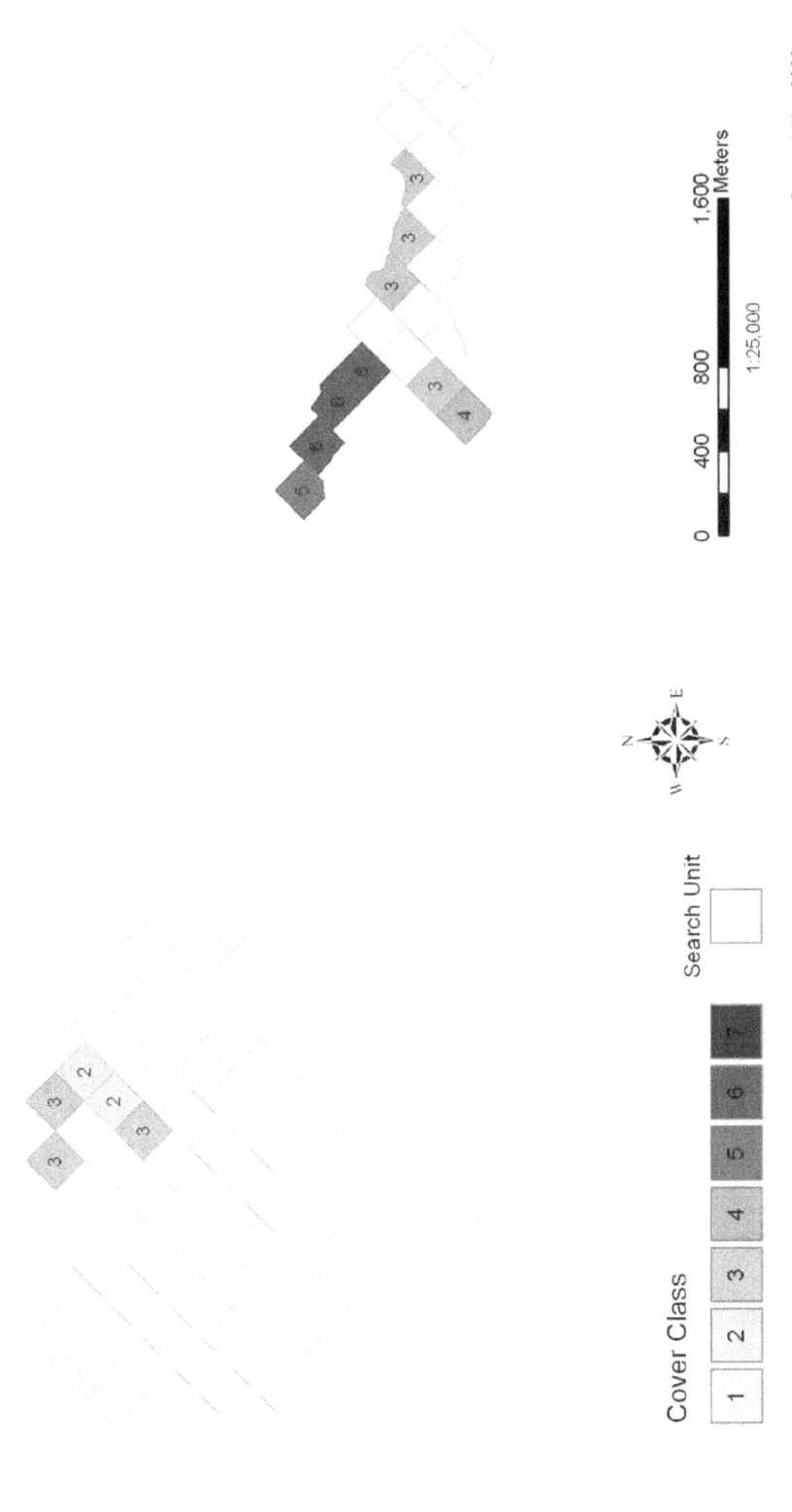

Microstegium vimineum

2009

Cover Class

Search Unit

Figure 5. Abundance and distribution of *Microstegium vimineum* (Nepalese browntop) at Big Spring Pines Natural Area, Chubb Hollow, Long Bay Field, and Long Bay at Ozark National Scenic Riverways, 2009. Cover classes are as follows: 1=0.1-0.9 m^2, 2=1-9.9 m^2, 3=10-49.9 m^2, 4= 50-99.9 m^2, 5=100-499.9 m^2, 6= 499.9-999.9 m^2, and 7 ≥ 1,000 m^2.

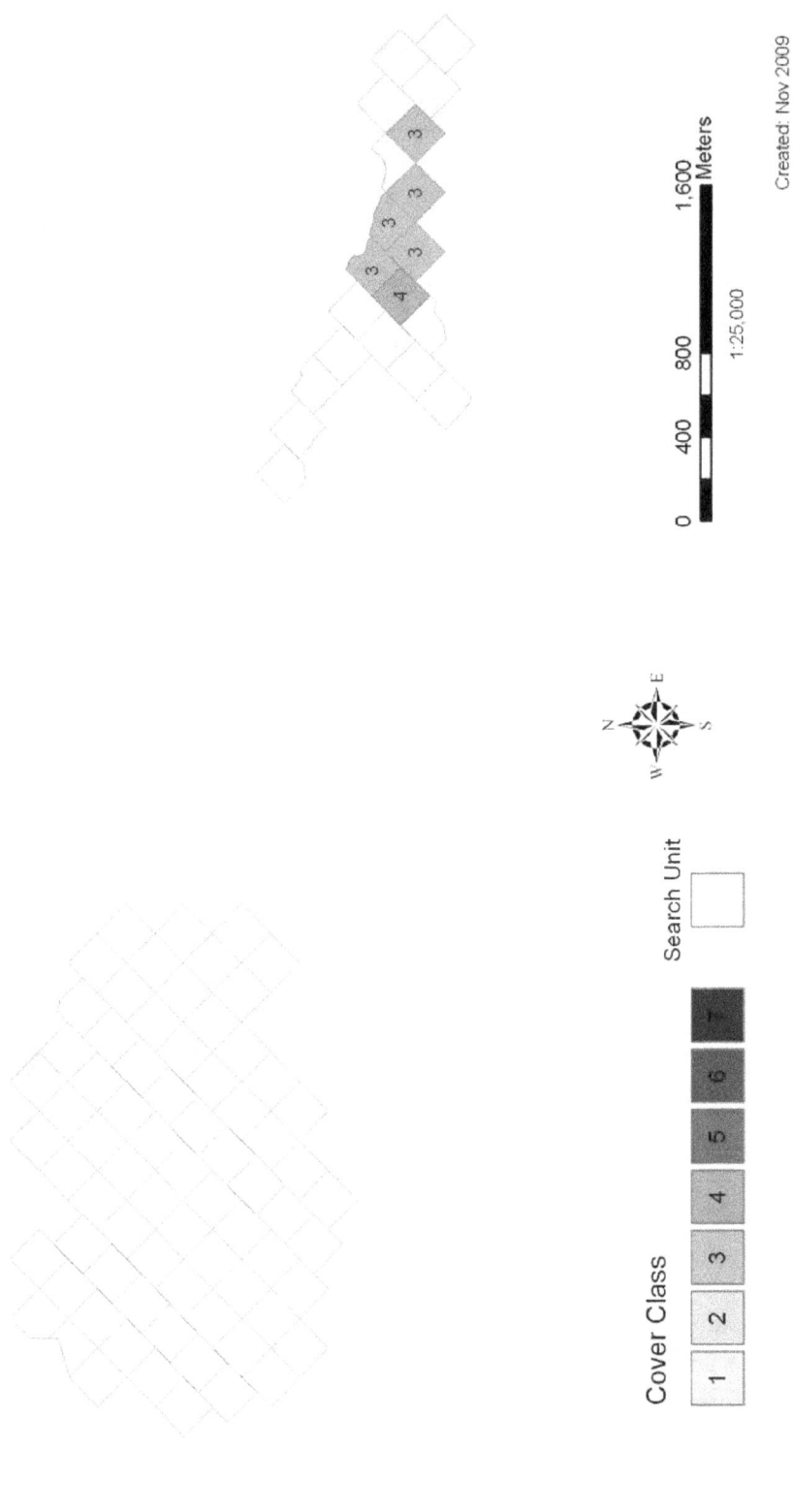

Poa pratensis

2009

Figure 6. Abundance and distribution of *Poa pratensis* (Kentucky bluegrass) at Big Spring Pines Natural Area, Chubb Hollow, Long Bay Field, and Long Bay at Ozark National Scenic Riverways, 2009. Cover classes are as follows: 1=0.1-0.9 m², 2=1-9.9 m², 3=10-49.9 m², 4= 50-99.9 m², 5=100-499.9 m², 6= 499.9-999.9 m², and 7 ≥ 1,000 m².

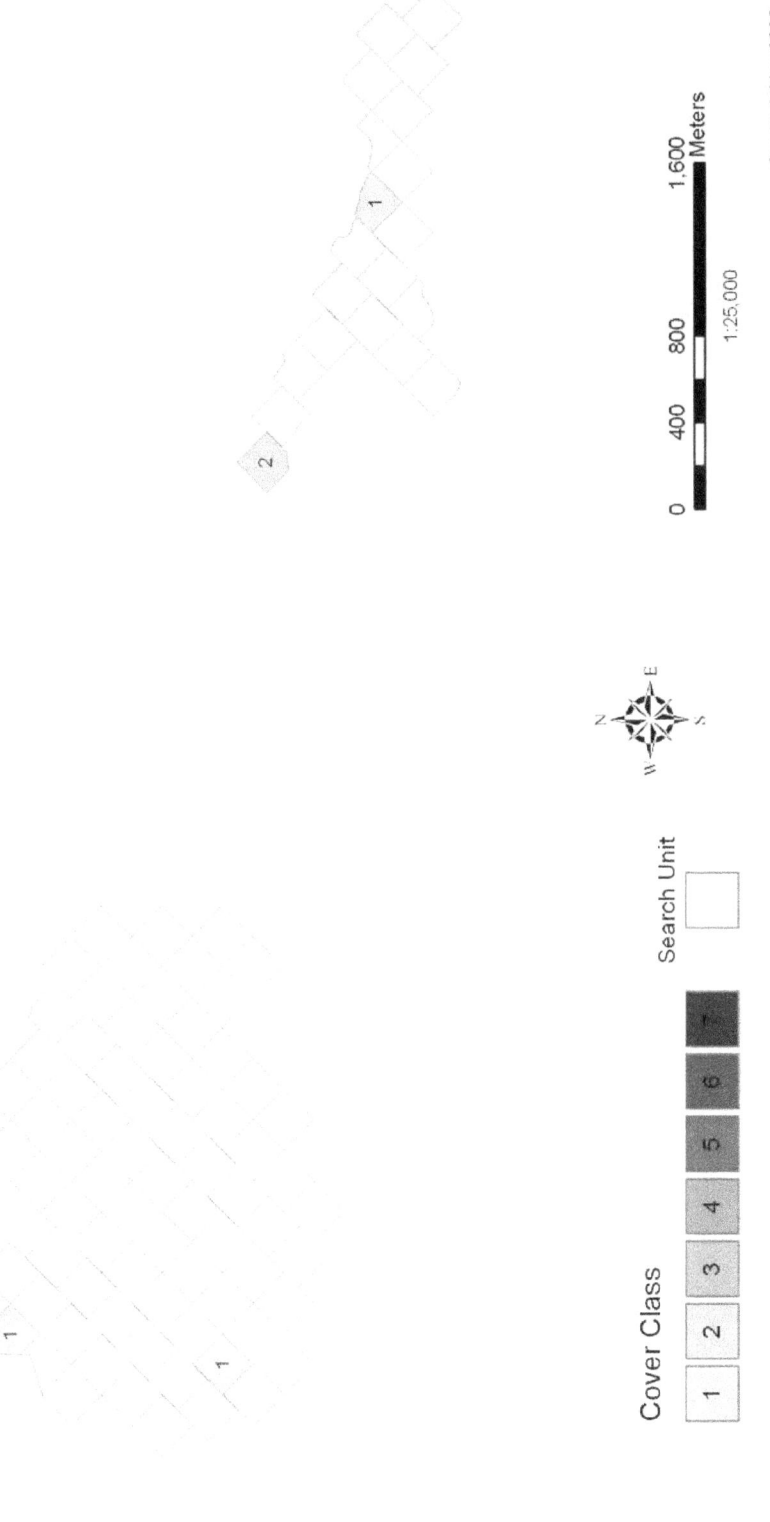

Rosa multiflora

2009

Cover Class

Search Unit

Created: Nov 2009

Figure 7. Abundance and distribution of *Rosa multiflora* (multiflora rose) at Big Spring Pines Natural Area, Chubb Hollow, Long Bay Field, and Long Bay at Ozark National Scenic Riverways, 2009. Cover classes are as follows: 1=0.1-0.9 m^2, 2=1-9.9 m^2, 3=10-49.9 m^2, 4= 50-99.9 m^2, 5=100-499.9 m^2, 6= 499.9-999.9 m^2, and 7 ≥ 1,000 m^2.

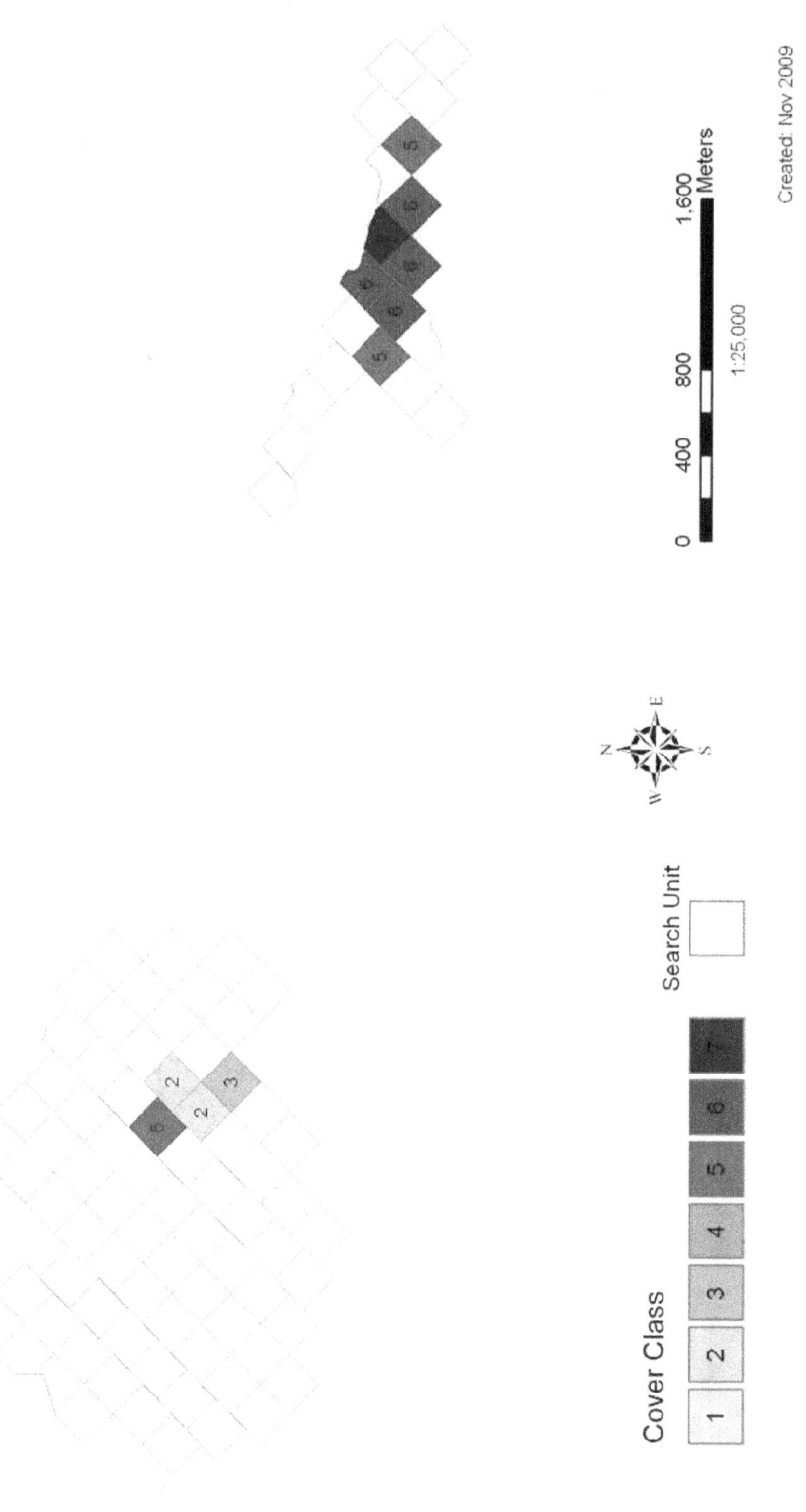

Sorghum halepense

2009

Cover Class

| 1 | 2 | 3 | 4 | 5 | 6 | 7 |

Search Unit

0   400   800   1,600
Meters

1:25,000

Created: Nov 2009

Figure 8. Abundance and distribution of *Sorghum halepense* (Johnsongrass) at Big Spring Pines Natural Area, Chubb Hollow, Long Bay Field, and Long Bay at Ozark National Scenic Riverways, 2009. Cover classes are as follows: 1=0.1-0.9 m^2, 2=1-9.9 m^2, 3=10-49.9 m^2, 4= 50-99.9 m^2, 5=100-499.9 m^2, 6= 499.9-999.9 m^2, and 7 ≥ 1,000 m^2.

The NPS has organized its parks with significant natural resources into 32 networks linked by geography and shared natural resource characteristics. HTLN is composed of 15 National Park Service (NPS) units in eight Midwestern states. These parks contain a wide variety of natural and cultural resources including sites focused on commemorating civil war battlefields, Native American heritage, westward expansion, and our U.S. Presidents. The Network is charged with creating inventories of its species and natural features as well as monitoring trends and issues in order to make sound management decisions. Critical inventories help park managers understand the natural resources in their care while monitoring programs help them understand meaningful change in natural systems and to respond accordingly. The Heartland Network helps to link natural and cultural resources by protecting the habitat of our history.

The I&M program bridges the gap between science and management with a third of its efforts aimed at making information accessible. Each network of parks, such as Heartland, has its own multi-disciplinary team of scientists, support personnel, and seasonal field technicians whose system of online databases and reports make information and research results available to all. Greater efficiency is achieved through shared staff and funding as these core groups of professionals augment work done by individual park staff. Through this type of integration and partnership, network parks are able to accomplish more than a single park could on its own.

The mission of the Heartland Network is to collaboratively develop and conduct scientifically credible inventories and long-term monitoring of park "vital signs" and to distribute this information for use by park staff, partners, and the public, thus enhancing understanding which leads to sound decision making in the preservation of natural resources and cultural history held in trust by the National Park Service.

www.nature.nps.gov/im/units/htln/

NPS 614/101124, February 2010